UPKEEP

Also by Sara London

The Tyranny of Milk

UPKEEP

Sara London

Four Way Books
Tribeca

Library of Congress Cataloging-in-Publication Data

Names: London, Sara, author.
Title: Upkeep / Sara London.
Description: New York, NY : Four Way Books, [2019]
Identifiers: LCCN 2019004733 | ISBN 9781945588396 (pbk. : alk. paper)
Classification: LCC PS3562.O48815 A6 2019 | DDC 811/.54--dc23
LC record available at https://lccn.loc.gov/2019004733

This book is manufactured in the United States of America and printed on
acid-free paper.

Four Way Books is a not-for-profit literary press. We are grateful for the assistance
we receive from individual donors, public arts agencies, and private foundations.

This publication is made possible with public funds from the
New York State Council on the Arts, a state agency.

We are a proud member of the Community of Literary Magazines and Presses.

The space we stood around had been emptied
Into us to keep, it penetrated
Clearances that suddenly stood open.
High cries were felled and a pure change happened.

Seamus Heaney, "Clearances"

For Dean

And for my mother, Susanne London

In memory of my father, Marshall London (1929–2012)

Contents

4 A Plain Path

Notes

1

Fugitive You

Breakfast with Martian on Election Day

It's not eggs that scramble me into day,
but the lowly oat,
crop of cool
moist climates, hoary as Bronze Age
caves, heart-pal—this
weed-flake wheeling
feverish through boiling water,
going thick and pale, bubbling
an unastonished

waltz. Our word *love*
was not intended for the cereal's
slow wrapping
of the wood spoon, or the steam
sucking on the pot.
(Too quaint,
some might say, porridge,
too hot-water bottlish;
in bed with booties,
storybook and thumb.)

How do you
do it, start the experiment—
gas up, each day, anew?

Old powder-hair George,
President Uno from Popes Creek
plantation, sowed the grain
at Vernon's mount
(well, his slaves did);
our confederate first.
Not the first man
to switch foes, nor harvest
victory amidst losses,
nor find that partisanship
sullies the mood.

Who is your Father?
Was he
reluctant,
too?

Hot cereal hardly
spared Goldilocks her fright,
though it gave orphaned Oliver
some added grit; drizzle it
with syrup from the giving maple,
drop in nuts, and the viscous,
punctuated muck of it

4

will spoon a salve of sorts,
a soft swallow for
beginning—

After breakfast,
soak the pot for the day, and—

    as the human skin thickens (or thins),
    as veins (blue-green like you)
    pulse out fuel and CO_2,
    as the colon drums
    forth the sediments—
    as all the body's instruments
    ply the hours and the soul
    strains to
    harvest rare light
    from the world's one loose tooth—

by then, the pot's aluminum will have grown
an inside skin, that, when peeled back
and discarded like molt,
will leave the scrubbed metal

pristine, reflective of
the late sun's useful
rinse. Mind you,

I'm just one
kind of American
at dawn (and dusk).
Don't be fooled,
or eat anything
that might tax
or change
the misty eloquence
of your alien
silence.

Teaching a Martian to Swing

Vision in these parts seems
to be narrowing; "global"
has its paradoxes. Eating is still
the measurement of a day.
Hunger, money, news. Knowledge
is valued, though we argue
about what types and how much.
We have triggers for this,
triggers for that. Wounds
and fears. How to explain?

At night you cast your noble
viridescence against the
whole of darkness—I've
probably walked right through you
on my way to the kitchen
for water or applejack
when I can't sleep
and my mind turns
to the simple tips I might share:
for instance, pumping
your glow-stick legs
in small increments at first;
hanging on, gripping hard

as you lean back and climb
the air on the schoolyard's
chain-hung plank-chair.
(The links will sing from friction,
grass and dust will perfume
the tug and puff.)
Pluck the day, as the idiom instructs;
you've come quite some distance
not to try this classic old pastime
before you make your meteoric
way, ablaze betwixt the stars
on your voyage back
to a chattering fringe of hues
that awaits fugitive you
and your hologram gifts.

Desire (why else would you
come?) carries a price here on Earth.
What I can't get over
is your kind of patience,
which seems tonight a little like
love. But I think (am I wrong?)

there's merely a pulse of minty
vapor, no blood at all
in your dreams—

or maybe you've touched
the shield of me, flesh,
skeletal ridges, or felt the heat
my skin releases against
the flurries of solitude; perhaps
you, too, have noted it, when
you slip your volcanic slopes
and we collide as nighttime
migrants, so unlearned in the
charter of our missions.

Rain on the Red Planet

We've learned that your valleys, too,
were chiseled by runoff, wet
air uprushing rust-red ranges, then
daggering down as snow or rain;
it's a hard rain's a-gonna fall—
and fall on your ancestors wafting
aloft in reams of drenched, unhurried
night, embryonical as jellies
blooming their own bodily
umbrellas. (Always there's a
prop we humans cling to.)

In Poland, circa World War II,
umbrellas, the wounded collapsed,
were brought to my neighbor's matka,
who mended the trunks and ribs,
glued Lucite or rummaged up
handles of wood. If mangled,
she straightened. If ripped,
she patched. She telescoped steel
to the cotton dome, until they
onioned once more above the bowed
heads of the hurried living;

and at the pump in the village square,
the beards of Jews piled up
on the cobblestones—soldiers
shearing off daven-stroked clumps
(earlocks, too, were snipped,
set aflame, refashioned as air)—
and flustered Zofi, just eight or nine,
dropped her sloshing bucket,
smashing her smallest toe.

At home, her matka bandaged
the toe in bread; it's what they did,
Zofi said. Winters so cold that ice
muzzled the pump's confounded mouth;
only the hardy made it to the river.

Beyond your perished currents
floats a rusty, atmospheric dust
rendering the reddened eye
we peer into. It pulses out its Hubble
riddle of gelid depths, and we,
like some blue-eyed son, gaze

through epics of mourning,
straining to drink your ancient rain.

"Cats and dogs" we say
when it falls as fiercely as this—
downpour and dusk doling out
another day's ending; somehow
Earth launches us, still, dark hours
hence, so we rise into soggy dawn
with our clanging earthly terrains,
our forest flames, our oceans that
nurse on cerements of ice.

Martian Twilight

My father liked sucking marrow
from Sabbath dinner's stripped

chicken bones, to my mother's dismay.
A doctor, he said it was blood made

savory, could strengthen our elbows
and knees, though we weren't

convinced. But one time he brought us
a steel hip socket, a sampler *acetabulum*,

heavy and peculiar across the landing
pads of our small palms, and we saw

how the solid plastic capsule of
femur swiveled in the pelvis's perfect

skeletal cup. In the chapter on human
grief, you'll find that with dreams

we exhume our dead without the mess
of upturned dirt. It's a neat trick,

the way the brain draws to the fore
and even salts what's dissolving

behind. I doubt your dead are tilled
into rows of dark unfarmed space;

our options seem so artless compared
with your simple grace of fade-out.

Be it joints or kids—we like the ring
of replacement, a way to go and stay

simultaneously. In the end, my father
cried often and freely, water being

what fills us up most. That we reduce
to dust is a thrifty lie. Our dead dwell

in divergence, and we follow them.
It's our custom—I'll set your stones

of speckled air on his mantel of granite.

Martian Melancholia

Maybe I have you all wrong,
your ethereal equanimity—
as if a transparency of blood
is the same as a lack of bile
or melancholy. We're
sculpted with it, as you've
probably noticed, our cells
hysterical in the body's seas
of devotion and doubt, our
blood a mulligan stew of self-
sedition. Yes, we do find
uplift, even in a backyard crow
scrabbling beyond the window
like Charlie Chaplin in his
here-there vectoring. We, too,
float, on inner wings along
currents of clocked assurance.
But sometimes the meaning
of our very clothes dissolves
as we tend to this or that;
our stones of pocketed
sorrows could surely
sink weightless you.
Many here think nurture

is the default nimbus
of why and because.
And some of us carry
a limber refusal, a quiet;
maybe you've hidden it
in the hem of your
coat of light—this pain
that tends, in rhythmic
intervals, to bloom
its own protean cure.

2

Borderlight

Foter's Tog

Whether you came because
I summoned you, as if to

an audition, or you drifted in
on your own wind's singular

script will never be clear,
but there you were, your old

handsome self, '70s hair
backswept, a little silvered,

and of course I hugged you,
though you couldn't lift your

arms much, buttoned into that
cindery, immigrant overcoat.

Your eyes were rimmed raw
from winter gusts, or the loop

of dreams—the skin so
thin there, where the soul peers

out, spilling its blue pools
before retreating again.

It was all backwards;
Mom had left you, as if

by divorce, moved on,
and your face was lit, flushed

with defeat. The arena, though,
was grand, an empty,

modern theatre, all too
silly now—just us, unfunny

father and daughter at center
stage. Desire couldn't have

moved your feet.
In the wings, was it Gratitude

issuing no lines or cues
for me at all? Just this

dream of our greeting,
so brief, in the borderlight

before daybreak.

Burial

How oddly we craved it,
the itchy grip of the gritty
grave, the cool body-hug
beneath the surface sizzle,
and the best part, the graphic
magic of the head, severed—
a face afloat on a sand
sea and still happily gabbing.

That dreamed-up violence
drove our ceremony,
our industry—a commune
of small tanned hands
slapping, tamping—all for *me*
(the interim dead alive
in a reign of perfect charade,
giving granite the toe test),
interred a while, now wiggling
like a seal lodged in a loaf
of turf, now barking out—*"Help!*
Help me!" and they,
the gleeful mini-morticians,
having fled as you failed

to break your grave—they'd
have galloped off to the surf
that licked at prancing legs
as if they were sugary
stallions, and you,
crying now, snot-lipped,
were dead.

    But always
you found your sandpaper
stick legs and staggered out,
relearning how to stand
and whom to be—always
merely who you were—
and still you swallowed that
mystery grief all uncoiling;
your fire-sprung feet
foisting thighs, belly
and nautilus self back
to the spank of waters,
while Mom and Dad, all
the shore's splayed subjects,
plainly vain in postures

of final defection, grew
sun-damaged and dull,
serenely dreaming—
these dead saved
to the world.

Kiss

All day my father complained
of the noise.
Today they took it down,
that massive elm across the street
(unproclaimed family crest),
cut down and carted away
in a yellow truck.
On the lawn below these turret windows,
hands in his sweater pockets,
he's walking over to inspect
the job. Still with his morning moodiness,
his gait is unusually stiff
but he bends from the waist like a boy,
draws a hand in circles
over the fresh cross-section,
thinking of the years,
a hundred, easily, spent
in perfect spangles of wood,
rimmed reminders
of old nests. And when he
stops with the stump behind him,
for a moment I worry
he'll sit down on it and look ridiculous
and old. This morning when he snapped

over breakfast I knew it wasn't
only the noise—the gnarling argument
of the saw drowning out the birds,
the scrape of silver against our plates—
but the season's leave-takings,
the air thinning in the ticking house.
Now he looks up, sees me in the turret,
waves and heads back over,
the longish graying hair he combs straight
back lifted comically by the wind.

They're new, these things he takes time for,
fills the feeders in the yard,
watches the cat. He'll even climb
two flights to watch the sun go down
from this empty room. He rarely came up
when I lived here, where we slept—
my boyfriend and I, teenagers
anxiously testing his reticence.
But one night, one midnight, he did come up
and stood with his back to the jamb
to tell us, too quietly,
that he had come from frantic hours
in a police holding room

with a woman, a patient of his
who had driven her daughter
out after dinner,
shot and killed her
behind the synagogue.
He lingered a long time in the room
absently scanning my strewn clothes
and sheet music, answering our questions,
talking slowly about the confusion, the husband,
the other children at the house,
his patient he couldn't calm.
And all because the daughter
was returning to Boston
where her lover,
a Jamaican man, was waiting.
And before he went down,
his eyes red with exhaustion,
he kissed us, both,
almost absentmindedly.

I hear that rare rhythm
of his hard shoes on the stairs—
familiar stranger that he is
to this room—he won't notice

the huge gap in the foliage,
the unblinking lake, or beyond,
the Adirondacks' rolling dips
and rises. He'll pause
to catch his breath,
ask what he can carry down.

Upkeep

It wasn't the fleet Arabian I'd dreamed of
racing through the grid of our Santa Clara

County development, but my father's
Mustang had ample horsepower,

and it ripped open the morning so loudly
the neighbors bled complaints. Which

made me love him more, the man who'd
inherited the fastback from Uncle Bobby

who'd slammed his prized plane of the
same name nose-first into Mojave oblivion.

In middle age, Dad had the navy body
repainted a blinding carmine zipped

with stripes; not an obvious fast-car man,
but an old-school house-call doc, hardly

home with his seven kids. He diagnosed
problems of the human hinge, bad

bones, but the flu and hearts, too—
a fix-it man sometimes chasing his own

repair. Before dinner, we'd wait at the
end of our street for a lift, his torque

the long day's last mad cure. Years later,
he worried much older wheels of faith

and prayer, and wept often. But his
Mustang sits high and dry with its

vines of rust and racked-up myths
on cinderblocks in the carriage barn,

and each time I haul garbage to the bin,
I see it perched there—like a caged,

exotic cat my mother can't part with,
dull without its howl and swipe,

a sphinx devouring the cracked wood
ribs of chairs, sparkless lamps and tarps

my father stored in its night-black bucket
seats when the car quit. His faith faltered

in the end only for bodies unfit for engining
forward. For matters of upkeep, he left us

lists, small desires recorded in a slowed
man's racing scrawl.

Mind of Winter

Manners and sunshine get you nowhere.
The clock noshes you to the quick so slowly
it's as if the unmaking itself is a myth.

So when you beg, please, *please,* we can only thank
the gutting, the shut-down that punts soft crumbs
through your colon-eel undulant on its nowhere

junket. We hoist you up because up is direction.
Your heels float on the pelt but god knows where
knees go, not I, you, not your son, *who?* your—

son of a gun! You, Father, stare from some gas moon,
a snowman molting misgivings—oh please, *help me!*
a hand slapping down like a starter flag—go, *go,*

will the snow ever stop or the rolling that's
rimed you—we dart everywhere for the carrot,
so sure we once were—Where's your hat?

Between the Dead

Their manners
are impeccable;
they never interrupt,

are cowed or cruel;
the right of way
is always ours.

They are discreet,
unlike the struck stones,
or leaves overhead—

a thousand pendants
of jaunty golden light,
some, like jaundiced

dreams, dropping slow.
A vast wheezing
engines the air, lofting

oceans. Saturday's
cars on crisp missions
sail past, fathers

unfrothing—skreeks,
whistles and tats
in the firs, the incising

of squirrels fattening.
Unsung Sundays spool
out. I walk between

the dead, righting
spilled plastic pots
of blooms purpling—

bending,
          straightening,
practicing.

The Wonder Book of Do You Know?

And now the answer
lies in the field, the harvest

once hand-by-hand heaped
                    to cushion the sleeper,

                    bedstraw, *Galium*,
with its tiny hairs
                    that "hook and cling," cleave
inside the coarse ticking,
so the mattress
                    doesn't slump
like a swayback,
                                        Galium greening

the hedgerows, small white
                                        star-blooms
            unsquinting

among the stiff,

            aparine stems, narrow leaves

arrowing up

frayed; common bedstraw rising in bogs, fields—

boreal, woodruff, catchweed,
                  coach-weed, sweet-scented, and goose grass. How

would you have made room for such tufts

       in a head

          so stuffed with dying?

Did you know

that sacks of river-filled goatskin,
in ancient Persia,

        made waterbeds for the original hippies?

          Egyptians piled palm boughs.

Romans had reeds, hay or wool,
                  feathers for the ruling few.
It seems anything

with a ghost of spine was used

(before affordable fluff):

      — pea shucks shoved
            into sewn cotton sacks
      — horsehair
      — strands
      — reeds

      gatherings to bear the body's
feet, pelvis, head,

pounds, like yours, of regret

or prayers or dreams
      swallowed up in the river
by a plague of frogs, so

      washed up you seemed

            on your high-tech pad,

a rectangular grid of little lungs

                                        pumping
to keep your backside skin
            from splitting (though it did)

as hours thinned it
                  and thinned, husking
                              you, until you
were the hours

clocked on your wrist,
(expandable silver band

      slipping along the papyrus
scroll of forearm) conducting half-songs,

                        over and over your notes

asking the hour, blue eyes buoyant

for more—   *What time?*
                              "Did you know

what finally standardized time
            in America?"

I'd learned it
on the radio driving up: Trains—
                     schedules of arrivals
and departures
      synchronized from city
to city, north to south, east,
                 plains, peaks, desert, canyon to coast, across
     rivers, sleeper cars
          shunting dreamers,
        hunger
and sleep
along
      diminishing tracks,
             bedstraw waving blind
along rails,
       nails rising.

   Bedstraw, then box springs,

then winter boxes,

     your Israelite bed of freshly beveled pine
pillowed in needles of balsam,
     under heaps

of New England snow.

(Sister covered you
with a quilt, you know, before the stone was cut—
perfect piecings,
by drifts, perished.)

Did you know

spring is an iron engine
chugging its surplus load

of seeds too damn
slowly east,
migrant chaff floating,
common weed rooting   everywhere,
red veins
plunging
and rushing up
as cleavers
of memory,
shucks and rushes

supplanted by memory foam—

Yes!—

poor old *stickywilly*,
                    bedstraw, now merely
                              tincture of syllables in wind, so many
tongued types: licorice,   shining,   fen—

And before you sealed yourself in,

          or out?

                    I would have asked another,

                    the kind of random

question
          you'd have tried
on me,

and answered: Bedstraw

          was good for ladies' hats too!

          —I might have

guessed torches, thinking

flames that

      when all goes dark

      illuminate what is
close,
      and from very far away

mark arrival

    or return.

A small star hoarding the oxygen.

    Bare ground

bedded shepherds who
gathered up their feet
for fetal heat or stretched
beneath stars, sleeping heads
fast to simple stones.

Nowhere
in the Wonder Book does it say—

all this time you
            have slumbered—already

            it is time
to awake.

Yahrtzeit

1.

It was a metal
folding chair, the kind
for latecomers,

its slight gray frame
hidden by the fasting
figure collapsed in it—

my father mourning
his mother,
beard shivering

into the silver flurries
of middle years;
once Hollywood

handsome, he
prayed through
knobby sorrow

like some Bowery
boy crumpling,
knees curbed at a

contingent edge,
black shoes like
old slow crows.

Nanny's plain pine
box was a blonde
surprise of grains

and knots floating aloft
in the anteroom;
it hung there like

a question we kids
clumsily hefted
as he shuffled out,

a stranger moldering
into morning and
savage sun on snow.

2.

The simple
stool I unfold
by his side

will do—it has
come down
to sitting.

Out his window
large white flakes
cling to flanks of

trees, a fence, the road's
ghosts. There's
ticking on the

window, the same
notes of unmanicured
nails counting

nothing and all
on the polished
plank of

a bedside table.
After,
weathers

came to whisk
me away
from myself. How

cloudlike I went,
scudding into
new accumulations

through two
winters. Then the second
August came—

hard, trammeling
rains, nightfall, and
crickets sawing

their taut guts,
tuning and tuning
toward day.

The Gale

Even the floor planks are huffing heat,

popping wood hips

no longer loving their joints.

Moisture swells the sponge air

and seas hang

in charred cauliflower bladders

giant over the town's tinder

roofs of late June.

In an attic room

a book's pages madly wave

at the fan blade's drilling,

fiction's colloquy

so windy and clarifying, tossing

the flailing *whys* of her

father electing,

one fall morning, to gather up his legs

day and night—

to leave them forever aloft

in their languor;

the pelvis became a mortar

chafed by the pestle of days,

soft in surrender

to the body's kitchen,

cupboard by cupboard

closing down. This, finally,

was his grandest chore.

 —And she milled pentameters in their walks
to and from the clinic of magic juices.

 —And mighty was his mandible for the
meats of the Israelites: But he closed-up shop

  with a mouth open empty

of psalms.

  Now the attic, steaming

with summer heat,

  is crock-potting his heirs stewing there;

  they, we, are the salted ribs

  in a century's house;

his daughter lies sun-fevered,

touching the cool forehead

of each lettered page, waiting

for the storm, *the invasion*

of garrulous pails

and voluble buckets,

for the gadding about

of brat winds in broken light,

the banging ladles

of land and tribe.

Braid

One moccasined toe at a time,
she descends the stairs,
lips quick in conversation with
shadows, her cumulus hair so
strangely combed out that its
weather confounds—thick
mists of it hovering past breasts,
down eight decades of a still
girlish spine, and she asks
Will you braid it?

My tripartite sorting brings
sighs—the twisting portends
composure, routine. Her pluck
is returning, lung by lung
for autumn's measures;
she roams with a thick-glassed
wand over newsprint, quick
to weigh the world, weary
of lingering "springs";
novels reorder her world's
ways; she makes lists—
groceries, gifts, and climbs
like a kid to water ivy that

stains the Victorian planks
below with its ample
over-drips.

And she drifts,
in dimming rivers of him,
who rowed an Old Testament
current, and liked locks neatly
shorn. But it's no rabbinical
dust with which she dialogues—
her syllables flicker in the quiet
rooms' motes like happy heathens,
while harder memories hole up
in the mind's cornices by day,
blading bat-fast into her
nighttime stirrings.

Her braid keeps for a couple of days
before stray sections alter
the mirror's map, inciting her
fingers' plunge into regions
she rakes through, until
fibers rise in clouds that softly
sock her in—

It's a kind of mock heaven
she steps with, from which she fishes
for daughters and earthly design.
So we weave, obedient, over
and under, carefully recrafting
the tether, refashioning a child's
greed for another go at lessons
in leaving, toward seasons
unsanctified coming on.

Acts

Let me tell you
about the dead. They
are different from
you and me. They
are dispossessed
of opinions earlier
than we, and it
does something to us,
makes us hard where
they are now soft
earth, cynical where
they are honest dust.
In a way, unless you are
dead, too, it is difficult
to understand: They
have less currency
but vast luck. The March
sun doesn't ask
for their attention
to the labor of the day,
the moon requires
no toil by night.
The marrow makes

new tunnels
to somewhere.

So when
you go between
cities, remember, the
one who feeds, spoils, schools,
frightens and excludes you,
has another notion
of the ice or the grass
or the different dead.
When you dangle
your legs in the river
and the fickle current
threads through toes
long ago toweled dry
and tickled one
by one, lean and drink
the face that swims
in place, drool
again unabashedly,
say boo before
he gets to.

Cemetery Craft

There is a sphere defined—
not by the city's finite fencing
that holds the dead in (as if
mixing the traffic on macadam
with the bone trust underfoot
would undo us both, bring
souls careening to life
and the living too close to
the ones we once were).
The old gravestones are part
of the day's angular grace,
the place a safe parcel of time
that a small gray bird who
hops here unties like a charade
artist, again and again pulling
invisible strings through grass,
to branch, and sky, opening up
the possible. Impossible to name,
this acre; the heart aches—
inheritance is its own infinite
argument, but these granite
partisans aren't pathetic
caring things, know nothing
of brevity or atrocity, or how

crumbling the one walking,
how laughably cyclical her
sorrow. Here stand blind
guardians of the fictional sphere
a dirt road passes through.
Here, the lime grass is crowded
with buzzing flurries,
and grainy shadows turn
granite flesh to the slow slap
of sun—so, for a while,
the sting of the past and future
is lost to acts of impartial light.

3

New Weather

Loyalties

Chickens in the snow-bled
      furrows flicker like tired,
tawny flames, as spring
      drains the months' blues
and the dead float
      in new weather.
We know the species
      but can't decipher the genus;
never before did Father
      leave us for good.
So when sheaths up-prick
      from the garden clunch,
little green marines reporting
      on the subterfuge,
when soon the narcissus
      tilt their blitzed yellow
mouths to yawing heaven
      and let it rip, we take
sides, not meaning to,
      not thinking at first (at last?)
to apologize.

Reception

Ranks of wind-soused oaks
shake blue bars of shadow
across Rt. 47 and I'm imprisoned
for miles, fenders mud-tattooed
in the sloppy noon game.
The radio sneezes indecipherable
frequencies as I enter the flood plain
steering like a fiend and girdled
in grays, until the fuss fades
and I'm released into alluvial
sun, mooned by low-humped
cornfields oozing and ticking
with crows agleam in the hour's
blue oil. Thirst salts the window.
Will I wander, green, into work?
An elephant flaps a vast ear
and shifts the planet forward.

Clean Sweep

Only a DPW rookie would still be back-and-
       forthing it, in the town's industrial
sweeper, disk-brushes tornadoing, 6:00 a.m.,

       pistons rattatooing, crescendoing,
diminuendoing, again, the refrain—
       the bleeping beeping back-up coda

what the hell!—still in bed, you in diagonal half-
       sleep, me alert in my "I spy" psychosis:
Father dead five months, a ghost

       embedded, windless, locked—
see him sucked like a sail at his eyes,
       nose of papyrus, mouth rounding

oy—amorphous mistakes, his
       libretto of morphined encores—
(forgive for what?)—the

       contralto rattlebox, resounding
now in the town vacuum; now spritz-
       moaning the macadam scrub-song

of past precipitations, of sparing
　　　　nextness from previousness, breath
from the nosh—he halts, idles and, 6:20,

　　　　climbs down in his nice cap, begins to
shovel by hand a berm of sticks, leaves,
　　　　bent-up bees, scooping and chucking

the unsuckable, his body arcing birchlike
　　　　for every extant littered mite,
flying it to the front-loading

　　　　trough before hopping like wind
to his high, flashing cab—
　　　　where he thrusts once more into the clear

gust of his mission. So of course
　　　　by now I'm up with coffee, and
maybe it's just a boy's soft-throated Mike

　　　　Mulligan birling to Highland Avenue's
far end—bless them as they finally
　　　　caress new cuts of granite curbing and take

the far corner, leaving behind
　　　heaven, a burnished quiet that
bounces through window screen,

　　　and along our loved-up old
library table from which the *Times*
　　　casts back toasted crumbs

of cognition. But not so fast,
　　　meine liebe fraynd, allies listening:
Hear it?—that ghost-

　　　bleating, reversal pulse, a mechanized
plaint swimming the sea of green and
　　　paled backyards—back, the steady

measuring out of more
　　　morning—back, the gods
of to-dos and undoables, the gods of

　　　rain and phoning Mother,
of what-to-wear, to eat— Back,
　　　the complicated indelibility

of unknowable driven men.

Heaven's Bed

I stare up from steamed time
   at birds sprent in blind anticipation,
      part of a high-tide flock, sickle-winged
         and slicing through hunger. It's like a salting,

a feathered wind—heaven's bed
   finally shaken out. No decisions, they fly
   only by instinct with others, lean
      when they lean, lift when they lift,

land, lean, lift—propelled with spontaneous
   parameters: All is formed in the oneness
   of motion, position, velocity—the drift
   of the solitary one negated

by the collective, molecular synchronicity
   conducting the blue.

       —Whose switch and swerve
   is this dusk dinner-dance?

Am I a fast breaker, with a father now air
   in which all else happens?

Wayfarer

To say I sail would not account for my whereabouts,
or suggest the horizon is evident, or the north star
to be found. Wind rustles and retreats, and it's
entirely commonplace to find me plying

headlong into the froth of my own wake.
I do gaze. Distance is something I debate
as I dream, awake in ambient brine next to you.
Next to you I clang bells at the moon's milk-load

of wattage. I pay a medium toll for mixing up
stern and bow, mast and staff, suggestible (gullible)
and suggestive (evocative). Sank, sunk, etc., et alia.
But as I fumble metaphors in the lee of the licks

and in the Milky Way's way, your field tenders
its miracle magnet, tugging me through Cabo-de-Hornos blows,
          ensuring I skirt shoalings wending home.

Family Plot

There was a time when the dead stayed home,
sleeping their dark slumber in the back acres,
nursed in summer on coarse grass, clover and
Queen Anne's lace. Autumn drummed down
on the barn now emptied of Holsteins, mares,
the chickens in and out before snow sheared

by Vermont winds swallowed all sound.
Father, mother, sister and brother,
none now floating through dreams of the living.
Three lambs mark infants: their little loaves
of rashy granite now root-split; a woman gone
in labor, and moss mustaches fringing

the names of Old Testament kings and slaves.
The face of the house has slipped to one side,
stroke-like, wincing; and whipping the bequest
of blank hours, an old maple swats
her high switches, daylight flickering
in the heat of her fit. But what burns here

are foreheads we press to frozen kitchen glass.
No sugar, no batter, no grief left to feed with
cakes. No clemency either; next farm over,

a vintage Vermonter trains his owl-eyes
on us, suspecting plunder—but a gaze
tinted with wisdom: What cold hearth's ash

is just anyone's to stir, hum or chatter about?
In the rear-view, the back hill's stones teethe
on the ghost silks of clouds. A gust whirls
a dervish of white flurries, as if memory's
mendicant follows dizzy in our tracks.
We breathe the clearage of miles.

Feedback

for Rachel

That you've found him, our dad dead
three years, there in your truck's cab,
breathing, talking, patting your knee
with his chalky palm as you drive—
that you're nervous about the conceit, don't be.
I'm grateful he's just riding along
where we can see his blue-eyed acquiescence,
his ordinary pleasure, even his mild amusement
as the windshield recomposes the road home
and you've sealed yourselves into a linty pocket
on your way through mild weather
to nowhere special.

It's a fine, strange spring day. Does he say
your son is a good boy;
but gout is for the birds? Did you
imagine ice cream, but change your mind?
The signs (*stop, merge, exit*) he used to announce
so sharply to delay the end of the world
now perch like fat birds (red, yellow,
green) escaped from a crayola zoo.

I keep thinking there might be a Home Depot
somewhere out there for you, that giant orange sign
(gone the sour-smelling Guernseys, the tilting dairy barn,
the grand Vermont inheritance of brief corn),
and fanned-out rows of resolution, acres
of tools and fixes for walls, ceilings, floors
and lights that keep pinging out.
Maybe it's just more

duct tape you're after, royal mauve
for throw-rug stasis when the planet's spinning.
Go ahead while the sun is in suspension, get your
sugar cone before the nugget of golden belief is traded in
for night doubts. Keep the sprung throngs
of dandelion and clover petitioning
for your passage through the next fulgent flood-zone.
You, little Sis, on your maverick path to craft
the commonplace, be patient. Let him

do nothing special beside you a little longer,
even as the fuel gauge trembles in reserve, the chocolate
glops to your jeans and bloodies
the balding seat. And when he sings like that,
is his voice unwhirling out of wintry earth

like the hasty fiddlehead? Is he lifting
his lawless eyebrows now? How pink
are his prayer-cupped ears?

That it's not a dream, his drumming on the console—
his song a little too loud, a little too
long, his passion greater than God ever calls for,
as you loosen your grip and tap it out too,
a small reassuring code—
that's kosher; he's not out there
alone weeping his joy
on the disembodied wheel.
Along the way, maybe it happens; there's nothing,
old snow melt,
just seepage floating his sleep.

4

A Plain Path

Basta

Stitch in Time
is tired of saving Nine,

weary of forever
stepping up, peachy, alert

and prissy, the reliable fixer,
patcher, elbow-,

thigh-, knee-, ass-
rescuer, savior swift

with dowdy dexterity,
steely purpose and

doubling pep.
Oh so tired

of Time—the whispering
vast, the winds' splitting

infinities, the centuries'
eruptions, feasts

of error and woe. Stitch
is dying for a tacit

measure, a whole sabbatical
seamless and teeming

with sleep. Let them
do the binding—the straggling,

shaggy Nine—let the hinder
guard make their sluggish

way forward, heel-draggers,
bumblers who can beat

no one and can't even walk
the chalk, make them

tack a while in Samaritan
syntax, tending, nursing,

salvaging—so that Stitch
may dream the slip, love

the long drool in some
unplowed pasture, lick

the loitering of blessed
raggedy-assed lastness and

thrumming disaster. She's
earned it, she's spent her

spool, this cursed solver,
long-eyed and fibrous—

let her loose from this
curious contract;

the whip, it's beastly,
—it's time.

Banana and Batata: 3 Days

1.

They live together in the midnight
blue of the bowl, as if they know
the cliché—time is an infinite
thing, togetherness so very finite.
Theirs is an unlikely yet tender
tale of contiguity—the yellow
pod of pulpy sugar, beside the
starch-loaded boot, mimes a
vertical grin sheathed and sleek
in its rubbery lust. The stubby
umbilical-neck pokes above
the bowl's rim and tilts toward
the tuberous root's solid nub,
nuzzling it—the rustic one
is rolled so close its barrel belly
yins the yellow one's half-yang;
its rose embers glowing beneath
a dusting of dried loam.
You can nearly hear the winds
of commingled breath—the sigh
of a sweet, delusional sort of

stupor no house divided
could ever disrupt.

2.

To be devoured or discarded
matters not a tad—unpeeled
yet clad in a glaze of dream,
these two know of hope nothing,
nothing of racing blood's barbarian
reign. A much purer selfhood
chimes in these dumb snugglers'
vivid, present-tense repose.

3.

The yellow skin has freckled-up
with a gaining rash, and two whiskers
have sprung from the bulbous mate's
scarred breast—tendril-like,
the random feelers reach toward
the other's splotchy casing, as if

seeking some final, eternal charge.
But as with the sun's rise,
nothing can be done—a banal
morning theft alters the math,
and in the blue mouth of hours
the lumpy and leaden root tuber
(a staple in hard times)
grants its bare self
to the surrogate solitude.

Truro Seals

Some winking sphincter
surely pinched them out—
hefty slugs of the sea, one

shlumping back from shore
to water, the other, slothful,
soused on vintage sand.

Bones bind your
kind together within,
but what we see

is a tumid soul,
strange distended sack,
white splotched with patches

of black. You watch us
through fogged fraternal eyes.
We walk and talk, blue gams

scissoring a wide swath;
you loll, raising a foreflipper
in a yoga pose, whiskers sifting

the day's contracting sun.
We, too, are squeezed out,
splintery seekers of our

selves, laughing with luffed
mirth even as you mirror
our rubbery bullet of

doubt, lumping over
time's grains. When you
do that fat, swivel thing

in the surf, then slink, reticent,
below, sliding free from the
grief of elbows and knees,

do you know we search
for you, far out, like sailors'
wives, breath held for a break

in the whippled plain, squinting
for your sovereign
head, sure and sentient,

to crown, so we may
recompose our dream, turn
from the water's unraveling,

make our way home?

Letter to Seamus

Not to worry, I'm not searching
for a second father, though
the vision of Hibernian scoldings
squares with a sweet dream.

I'm still fit. I can lug a pail,
pat a haunch, slather a teat and
haul a wheelbarrow full of tossed
poems or tinctured manure,

wisp that I am, once hailed as
a mountain woman for my battle
with lobsters in an outboarded
dory. That victory's decades

dust now, but hear my hunger
motoring into a squirt of Atlantic
knots. What you write about
the trance, another words as "yes"

in a tossed bottle, another
terms a feast at the bottom
of memory furred by invention.
Virtue I'm never clear on,

mixed sod that I embody.
Dad's been dead a while now;
his ghosty blues still breaking
through the haze at my

command—brain-despot the
only thing, and that goes, too,
sloughing off like snow-skin,
but not yet! He did sorry stuff,

that was his canticle at the end—
a good heart going so unglossed.
No, not pattering after familias,
but an abundance of heather

to boot through, a dale, a hill,
a hail in shocking weather or
not from one who's made the
field a felt thing. Beware of

hunger that sails the ship,
the devouring bog swap
of a dreaming Sally;
I see you tip a ruddy squint

towards nothing frail for long.
Cheers, mate, on bringings
home, on islands as stepping
stones. Were my stride wide

enough and letters still licked
and ripped open, perhaps our
meeting would chance upon
unscrumbled peat, a plain path.

True Value

I don't know why I loved the tree of nails
with its tin containers holding spikey nests
of galvanized or ungalvanized steel, so
weirdly medieval, like a rough-forged fir.

It was always best to let the store clerk pinch
the nails with his smudged leather glove,
drop them into brown waxy bags promising
"True Value." Here, solutions were sold

in pennyweight. The aisles, for a child,
were stocked to dope the eye, all blinking
deliverance—from molten unknowns came
fixes flickering forward, cast, cooled,

screws and bolts, braces, chains,
brackets and plates—a map to rugged
purpose, or just artful scabs for a world
of scrapes. Chair backs detached, wobbly

stairs, newel posts split or missing—these
were dittos of our own undoings;
even the hickory heart of Dad's hammer
cracked. Did he just know to bring me,

or did I beg to come along? It took me
years to discover the cure-all hinge,
the "double-acting" kind, so doors could
swing; the coiled hinge-spring kept a

kicked door waving, like the one my
father, dead, nonetheless goes out and in.
(Funny how memory's hardware stays
greased to keep our ghosts from going.)

He'd agree it's good to keep practical
joinery at hand for when the flaps of a
house or box come loose. But I employ
this hinge—a "Stanley," just 1 x 2 inches—

for its wit of parallel spines, each spooling
stacked pins so you open an alloyed leaf
to the left, close it, then open (*voila!*)
to the right. He knew the quirks and limits

of clinging (and come snow, his time,
all but the firs had let go). There are days
that depend on such pedestrian repair.

New Worlds

for El Anatsui

The bottle tops I scrounged were smashed by hoofs
and tires, mere trash, but they lit up the rubble
with flashy script for foreign drinks—at age

nine I palmed the caps as pelf and imbibed Mexico
City's weirdly jazzed streets. I feared the saint-faced
boy with spuds for feet, who wheeled his body

by on a savior plank, zooming past Chiclet-
chanting toddlers twanging the shivery mosaic heat—
all day they shuffled their milktooth treats

through the fly-afflicted market. I still have the ink-
eyed don and doña, dropped from rocking crosses
and string-danced to tap the purses of tourists;

my brother got a gold-toothed beggar mask;
an eyeless white fox, bearded gray with decades
of dust, snarls over my father's dormant desk.

But, El, those crimped caps I left rustling in their
sack on the jet that flew my family home, they
were a loss I mourned at nine and even now—

yet now you've made some million lips so strangely
suck the beauty back, not the sizzling citrus
of Jarritos Tamarindo or Joya, but African

opiums, Niccolo, First Lady, Star Ponche,
like lost gold careening through continental space
beyond hope's gnarly-knuckled Allah, Buddha,

Christ or Adonai. This, a tangible art. I've gleaned
the story of your hands: Ghana born, youngest of 32,
you scavenged to reap meaningful luster, to touch

some shining, elusive thing—bending, pounding,
painting your cluttering path; what you found
was an earth of thirst, and you blasted diasporas

of tin and light, a kind of preening armor, across
dull-fleshed walls, as if myriad shields might link
all our tired little worlds. I think of the poet's urn

who spoke its radical mind on beauty, on truth;
your loud parades of rallying tongues, the sinned,
the salvaged, bells tingling blood's tributes here—

we pause, the merry drunk reminded. The heart's
pipes never yet wrung, old tubes, they play on.

Acknowledgments

My sincere thanks to the editors of the following publications, in which versions of these poems first appeared:

The Carolina Quarterly; The Common; The Cortland Review; El Anatsui: New Worlds (Mount Holyoke College Art Museum exhibition catalogue); *The Hudson Review; The Music of What Happens* (Orchard Books anthology); *Ocean State Review; Pinyon Review; Provincetown Arts; Quarterly West; Salamander.*

And my deep gratitude to these individuals for encouragement, insight, love and friendship during the making of this book: Dean Albarelli, whose devotion and steadfast support is foremost, and immeasurably inspiring; my mother, Susanne London (for so much more than her poetry genes), and my late father, Marshall London; my siblings, Rachel (for her discerning reading of a rough draft), Dan, Nomi, Saul, Rebecca, Linda and their families; Dinah Berch, my niece and expert website designer; Nancy Albarelli and family; Kati McDonald (who introduced me to Burkina Faso's poet emperor); Dorothy Antczak; Sam, Jenny, Catherine, Joyce and Bill Tager—my Provincetown family; Hutha Sayre; David Hamilton and Rebecca Clouse; Laura Gross and Charles Dellheim; Ann Beneke; Susan Seligson; Zofia Grygorcewicz, dear friend and neighbor; the Moushabeck families; Paula Dietz; Ron Koury; David Fleming; and Stacey Phillips.

A special note of gratitude and love to Carlotta Luke, for a long and nourishing friendship, and for her lyrical vision of East Sussex, England's vibrant fields ("Death by Flowers") on the cover of this book; Chris Luke (whose hands rise above those rapeseed blossoms); Giacomo, Roxy, Dylan and Ellen—my Truro family.

To Martha Rhodes, Ryan Murphy, Sally Ball, Clarissa Long, Noah Trammell, and everyone at Four Way Books—thank you for ushering these poems into the light.

Notes

"Acts":
The poem alludes to a noted passage by F. Scott Fitzgerald.

"Clean Sweep":
Meine liebe fraynd is Yiddish for "my dear friends."

"Feedback":
I'm indebted to my sister Rachel, whose short story inspired this poem.

"Foter's Tog":
Title is Yiddish for Father's Day.

"Letter to Seamus":
This poem was written the year before Seamus Heaney's death in 2013.

"Mind of Winter":
Title borrows from "The Snowman" by Wallace Stevens ("One must have a mind of winter / To regard the frost and the boughs / Of the pine-trees crusted with snow…").

"Rain on the Red Planet":
I'm indebted to Zofia Grygorcewicz for sharing stories about growing up in Dabrowa Tarnowska, Poland. *Matka* is Polish for mother.

"The Gale":
Title and quotes are from the short story "The Gale" by Bruno Schultz, author of *The Street of Crocodiles.*

"The Wonder Book of Do You Know?":
Title borrows from an early 20th-century British children's book series. The poem is dedicated to my late father.

"Yahrtzeit":
Title refers to the Jewish tradition of remembrance on the anniversary of a loved one's death.

Sara London is the author of *The Tyranny of Milk* (Four Way Books). Her poems have appeared in many journals, including *The Common, Quarterly West, Cortland Review, The Hudson Review, Poetry East, The Iowa Review*, and the *Poetry Daily* anthology. She teaches at Smith College, and has also taught at Mount Holyoke and Amherst colleges. Sara grew up in California and Vermont, attended the Iowa Writers' Workshop, and lived for many years in Provincetown, Massachusetts. Also the author of two children's books, she is the poetry editor at *The Woven Tale Press* magazine. She lives in Northampton, Massachusetts.

Publication of this book was made possible by grants and donations. We are also grateful to those individuals who participated in our 2018 Build a Book Program. They are:

Anonymous (11), Vincent Bell, Jan Bender-Zanoni, Laurel Blossom, Adam Bohanon, Lee Briccetti, Jane Martha Brox, Carla & Steven Carlson, Andrea Cohen, Janet S. Crossen, Marjorie Deninger, Patrick Donnelly, Charles Douthat, Blas Falconer, Monica Ferrell, Joan Fishbein, Jennifer Franklin, Sarah Freligh, Helen Fremont & Donna Thagard, Robert Fuentes & Martha Webster, Ryan George, Panio Gianopoulos, Lauri Grossman, Julia Guez, Naomi Guttman & Jonathan Mead, Steven Haas, Bill & Cam Hardy, Lori Hauser, Ricardo Hernandez, Bill Holgate, Deming Holleran, Piotr Holysz, Nathaniel Hutner, Rebecca Kaiser Gibson, Voki Kalfayan, David Lee, Sandra Levine, Howard Levy, Owen Lewis, Jennifer Litt, Sara London & Dean Albarelli, David Long, Ralph & Mary Ann Lowen, Jacquelyn Malone, Fred Marchant, Louise Mathias, Catherine McArthur, Nathan McClain, Richard McCormick, Kamilah Aisha Moon, Beth Morris, Rebecca & Daniel Okrent, Jill Pearlman, Marcia & Chris Pelletiere, Maya Pindyck, Megan Pinto, Eileen Pollack, Barbara Preminger, Kevin Prufer, Martha Rhodes, Paula Rhodes, Linda Safyan, Peter & Jill Schireson, Jason Schneiderman, Roni & Richard Schotter, Jane Scovel, Andrew Seligsohn & Martina Anderson, Soraya Shalforoosh, Julie A. Sheehan, James Snyder & Krista Fragos, Alice St. Claire-Long, Megan Staffel, Dorothy Tapper Goldman, Marjorie & Lew Tesser, Boris Thomas, Connie Voisine, Calvin Wei, Bill Wenthe, Allison Benis White, Michelle Whittaker, Rachel Wolff, and Anton Yakovlev.